I0585603

small town lazarus

Ashley Capes

small town lazarus
Copyright Ashley Capes ©2019

Cover: Vivid Covers
Layout & Typset: Close-Up Books

ISBN-978-0-6483957-7-5

Published by Close-Up Books
Melbourne, Australia

For Brooke

acknowledgements

Some of the poems in this collection first appeared at www.ashleycapes.com but additional pieces also appeared or are forthcoming in the following publications:

literally literary, the junction, p.s. i love you, lit up, wild (GP anthology), uneven floor, the bluepepper and *cordite poetry*.

Many poems, or versions of them, also first appeared on my Medium profile.

Thanks to the editors of the above publications for their support.

Special thanks go to Ivy Alvarez for helping me with this collection, in so, so many ways. I would also like to thank my loved ones for what has suddenly become twenty years or more of supporting my poetry.

contents

you again
admit one
pale wings
a million times
smaller and smaller
special occasions
risk
young pine
thieving light
ready? go
pink tickets
swoon
mark each other
tinkerbell

small town lazarus

come back grim man
these streets go rotten without your heavy
breath
to refresh;
the crisp silver frost
the halo
on eucalypt
the balm on burning litter
in bins
and the long croak of the crow, his
black flickering
across my window

there where I watch for you
& worry
that even your twig of spring
cannot galvanize me

but see how I seek you still
the crumbling whispers of dry earth
heaving,
the stunning suicides
of cherry petals

and all the flat moments, too
the carnival
right after
that final somersault
and the same dead-eyed

hours between town A and town B

if I find you can you tell me, will you know
exactly
what to do this time?
can you safely say
forever
in the kind of voice
that even our tombstones
will strain to hear?

fingers

the spider-woman has a script.
you can't deviate
or she eats your family or your favourite album.
her egg-sac looms over every meal.
you fight for whatever's on the table
with any tooth or nail
you can find.
her smile is glacial but you know where it ends.
if she falls asleep and you go outside to play,
that's it.
you're grounded in sticky silver silk
until she remembers to let you go back to work.
you sweat over every coin
and they shine as they disappear into her maw.
your only reward is more saliva.
some people don't have a spider
or so you've heard.
they have one of the three bears,
whichever one didn't eat goldilocks
and he gives his family honey and bees
to make more honey.
it sounds amazing.
of course, the bear knows the guy upstairs.
has a stay of execution
up his soft sleeve for emergency indiscretions.
the others talk about his button nose;
how cute it is, just a little cold to touch.
your spider has eight eyes to watch
and you never touch her.

not even at night, when she sleeps above the bed
after tucking you in, prickly hairs lingering
in the sheets.
you don't even think about touching her
because she has told you exactly
what will happen
to your fingers if you try.

no wild sky

after the tiny war I waged

no creeping flower, up between footprints
scent like a bullet

no wild sky
heaving telephone wires like skipping rope
or splattering
memories across windows

just a long, long vacancy

like a last motel
shrinking
against the slow onslaught of indifference
and crumbling
as thistles
march in to take possession.

a breath

yesterday my neighbours
were digging
and today
the fields still bleed petrichor
as the hissing song
of rain in grass
comes through the wire fence

and above, the sky cradles purple:

it hangs there just long enough
to settle
quite softly between
the spindly arms of my clothesline

and all through the evening
mosquitoes hover
over puddles
like stinging question marks.

city #1

when I say 'city'
I'm going to leave it at that so I can fool you,
lure you into a false
sense
that I'm talking about *your city*
even though I've never been
and won't climb swing jump or fly there either
so you'll have to pretend
I'm not actually talking about Melbourne
when I bump into head-set
suits
at the lights,
they've got their
I'm-saving-the-world-this-very-minute faces
on, complete with an
almost-shaven
look
good enough for Vogue,
or go with me when I wish I had a decent lens
for the graffiti
that's just sort of heaved across the walls
as if it'd time-travelled
with a hiss
to crash-land
in a 1990s rainbow,
or imagine it's really your favourite city
stained neon
with fast food, like the fat old spider
that lives in the corner

of the shed
and that no-one really worries about anymore
but probably should,
or take a leap
into the sound; buskers
buried alive
by
the righteous fury
of car horns
and arguments about who stole
the cigarettes
from who,
the ruffle of pigeon wings
like a hundred tailors
marching
or
early morning sirens
that leer
and moan, that transform
the hotel room
into a crime scene
even if you're only waiting for room service
innocently
waiting
if you don't mind
go along with me still
– if this was your city
would you notice the wind like a welterweight
going all Ballroom
with leaves of autumn-fire
or abandoned lottery tickets
ink running
splintering
sprinting
then

disappearing around the corner
to find only
the starving maws
of stormwater drains,
can you sit at a sidewalk cafe
and pretend
to like coffee *that much*
and wait for someone
and fool yourself
into thinking
everyone else
is at least a little curious about you
because you're
so calm
in a place
full of ricochets,
or is that too much conceit
because
on the other hand,
we both know
that here,
like everywhere else,
a thousand eyes
a minute
will skip over anything
that doesn't quite fit the romance
of the city
and afterwards,
the play-once-and-it's-done
highlight
reel
of concrete
glass
and tanned skin
is simply
gone.

whirling

the platform seems
to mutate
as
pink shadows
finally catch up
to every passenger, turning them
into pastel
silhouettes,
from the guy
waiting with briefcase
and mouth down on a cigarette
to the kids
clumped together
with their
ears bursting music
and the older lady
glued
to her shopping bags,
they
become
a long, thin museum
frozen
only for as long
as it takes
for the doors to hiss
and then it's right back
to the choreography of chaos
whirling
between bolted

furniture
and
maybe it's beautiful
the way
that for now,
everyone is going
somewhere different
together.

square goliaths

a little
trapped
but turning left
where the gutters glisten
and the crowds preen
and
for ants
crossing the street
it's a red sea, traffic lights like alien
invasions and horns making thunder
in many colours
cars
rumbling,
square goliaths
with windows-down and
drivers tapping
their long fingers in eternal
rhythms
of patience
or less
and some of them
only cracking the seal
to expel smoke
into air

glancing
perhaps across to the bakery
with its brass savouries
mincing about

behind the glass

and below each car waits
yesterday's puddles, they
have gathered
with such hesitancy,
as if having been
put up
to something unpleasant

so I step around them
and think
for just a moment
about slipping
down into
the mob-rule of debris;
leaves, bottle caps
plastic wrappers and cigarette buts
all rafting to the drain
and eventually
the sea-side
where swimmers
sunbathe
and I might too

but instead
it's nothing so fanciful –

just another
twenty or so steps
to my stop
and then
once I get home
you know that I know I can do it all again
tomorrow.

crash

it doesn't quite rain after the car crash
but the sky
just hangs there
flat
and still,
as if it's been unplugged

and we pass
so many cars lined up
to watch,
people standing
in the low
grass
just cut,
phones out
for I don't know what

and there's a rainbow
dripping
down
from above
and we imagine spirits
climbing the colours,
with no way
perhaps
to know
exactly what went wrong.

silvery ships

the sand stays mute
in its shroud of moth-wing grey
and ice-cream sticks
                    jut
free
like lost oars

and just beyond
the smooth light of morning
waves mass

as sea monsters
who long sulked in the ink,
with only the thin bones
of ancient sailors
to keep their company,
now thrash about

and prepare for spring,
clearing the seabed
with their tremendous fins
and leaving
the silvery ships
above
clinging
to the surface
by the tips of their barnacles.

monarch

the butterfly husk
is tiger-orange,
wedged between
grass blades
tallow with autumn

it's still dusty to touch

and its little antennae
are frozen
like twisted wire
with miniature
lakes of black
for eyes

and in them
I know,
I must loom so large
and so clumsy.

worn down

when I looked up from the desk
the afternoon had worn down
to a glowing nub
on the horizon
and a chill came with it, lurking
between one blink and the next
and even though
I was standing there, stuck deep
in the hush
it felt like I was just
passing through the moment
and god, I wanted
something
wanted meaning
but there was only a vague unease
to the aftertaste.

pretending that if I stop

a plastic bag floats by/great rents/howling/
there's so much wind it tangos the leaves of every
tree & seems reluctant to cross the floor/but
overhead the clouds just waltz by/soft peaks in
the sky/all those blues like a tailor's swatch/and
down beneath the hills the cows are chequered
picture-book style/they chew at tufts along the
old railway line where the rust is still smooth: it's
racing the river home & as fast as I pedal

I'll never catch it

never reach that humming freedom of engines
on the highway/they really know how to soar
& I'm stuck as some great stone/imagining that
movement is so easy/ so beautiful/pretending
that if I stop here/maybe/I'll catch them next
time around.

push back with air-conditioning

today light was weaponised
well before I woke
and it pushed down
hard
spreading
across the house and the driveway too,
it filled the car with its heroics
and put me in my place
give up
already
it seemed to be saying
and so I pushed back with air-conditioning

and for that 15-minute drive
I didn't really have to experience the season at all

instead, I reduced it to these lines
like
a thing remembered
and eventually remastered
instead, I played them over and over
even
the less triumphant reels
and the re-runs
cutting everything together
making another
Frankenstein's monster
from the little bits of truth that lingered:

searing sand
that set me and my friends to tap dancing
back when
every flavour of ice-cream was an explosion of joy
or the torture of vinyl bus seats
and the mile-long evenings
to go with the thunder of lawn-mowers
massing
up and down the street

little strips of what I maybe used to love
now replaced by my endless
grumbling
as summer becomes something to endure
and I know
in this moment, I have aged horribly.

still settling

1.

how   grass
    the long   sweeps itself
                up
       and
       takes its secrets
       away

       tiny exhales
    between
       dark mandibles
wind
       and last year's cigarette
    lingering
       with the still-settling satisfaction
       from that small-town heavy
       and
       his ride-on mower
    the saints
  echoing
    my disapproval as wind turns
every leaf into a mayday-signal

    scars
    build where they crash-land

    and blackened worms

come to my front step
            in frozen pirouettes
                        to flesh out their cemetery

it
happens   after   every   rainfall
and

there's no way to stop any of it

or save
the bits that don't grow back

2.

                                    before
there was   2 cent coin but   they
            a   turned
                                    such
                                    copper
                                    into
                                    the
                                    wet
                                    dream
                                    of every
                                    bank-fee
                                    manager

            and there's more
            down there
            of course,
            sweetening in the soft earth

more than ant eggs

in the hundreds or thousands

there's a single scale
there too
chipped from whatever's left of my empathy
a tendril of rubber
from the soles of my boots
and with it
the rhythm I never claimed to have
undergoing a pale petrifaction

if   the sun ever gets trapped
within the stalks

I'd like to visit
and get digging

3.

from down here
the tap's like the scaffold of a rocket
steely grey
pre-celestial
a slender Everest for the eye.

right before the first mosquito

first
steps into the evening
                    just cooling off
          in that moment
                    right before the first mosquito
                                        arrives
and ruins everything

          I cut the garden hose.

          as the tap squeaks
          a few final tears escape the faucet
          and run into green

     tomorrow, the golden mist
     that creeps across the fields
               will be a burning memory good for
     tough spots
               and possible paintings
                         or photographs
               I should have taken

               but

               just as powerful
               I think,
               is if I let it decay at its
               own pleasant rate

mulch
down and
feed me as if I had never eaten before.

cattle swelling

beyond the hills
there's cattle swelling,
hooves beating a nightmare-samba
and flies running about, washing everything
with their germs:
they send out
fetid signals
now
to slip between the rotting pillars of the day
and become nothing
but
detritus
after the things we loved,
simply
swallowed up
by a beautiful and
disinterested sky
so empty
and so blue, so
cruelly
blue
and unchanging,
when all anyone wants is a
few drops
for a few weeks –
just the supposed promise
inherent to winter
but instead it's mere 'prayers for rain'

coming in from the capital,
slinking into the kitchen
on dry
wi-fi signals

like a bloody curse

like the creak of straining rope.

fragile span

another morning
yet to be ironed
and so utterly innocuous
at first glance
but, how easy it is to waste
simply
because it looks just like the others

when I try to speak
there comes
nothing but a splash in a well

and, desperate
to make
something outlast this fragile span
I drag at the purse strings
of heaven, until its cherubs
come tumbling
down in an avalanche of wings
and rosed cheeks

and when they hit
they form a sad little row of clumps
like
things
left unfinished

until the rain comes and puts everything
to bed, and all around us

doors click
behind empty washing lines
and cobblestones
gleam
with sometime-secrets

nothing I can reach:

for I have made no gains
offered no
truths, comforted none with these words
least of all myself

and the statues are starting to slump
now
they're groaning
beneath the weight of resurrection
and exhibition, their faces
slick with tears
as here
comes the reaper, with gentle,
crumbling face and
measured, stately pace

and it never goes away—
that urge
that siren call
so insidious; I cannot
deny wanting to make the now
burn bright enough

to be worth saving
and as things fall out of focus
once more

I think I catch a glimpse
of Gabrielle making a fist, his head bowed
in a field of lavender
and mist.

the blue bird of unhappiness

everyone is living autopsy –
chests ripped open like butterfly-caskets
and secrets spilling,
wiggling free
with no way to hem them in

but you simply must share
to keep up
at least
until you can monetize

and even if they aren't
your moments
don't worry
you can turn that private conversation
between strangers
into the perfect loss-leader:

just swab it in bright colour
captions
to popcorn the audience
into smiling
and setting the phone down
after another few retweets,
feeling, no
knowing
really knowing deep down
that

I was just part of something warm and fuzzy

and you gotta share
so we know that you're still out there,
come on! shake it
already

oh – but I should say please be careful too
and don't forget that those

new pitchforks
can really
click

and that once you start

you can never really pacify a machine,
you can only feed it more
and more
until it becomes some great, sniggering oratory
that sucks down satellites

and pumps out
home addresses

but come on! look at this shit
it's the stocks all over again
only this time
without
the inconvenience of rotting vegetables

and it laughs and laughs
as it pirouettes
and spills its red wine on rented carpet,
and all throughout the house

the echo of hand-claps
set to the beat of 'celebrate'

will ring

and nothing, not a single thing
will think to stir.

start on a new name

you're getting that look now,
a desperation
born of the ever-growing distance
between fingertips

where what you miss isn't the actual
skin so much as the
possibility
of skin

and tell me, is it this, does the world now
chew up your best memories
and replace them
with passwords and usernames
and substitute voices for the clamour of mice?

you start on a new name
but the letters
go tumbling into the night,
coating the streets in old silver

and from the far smaller
spaces we're pushed into we still
reach out
to one another

with a stubbornness
sweet
against the nest of cables
hiding beyond the dark side of the screen.

when I become a thing

the world of things
wants me to collect enough things
so that when I become a thing
I will have left behind so many things
that people will remember me,
forced to spend
so much time having to sort
and pack my things
and trash some
and keep others,
some things growing new things
and yet more becoming the kinds of things
that make a splash
in op shop windows
twenty maybe fifty years after such things
have long outlived their uses
and transformed instead
into things
that only have value as things,
things only worth keeping
based only
on
their *future possible value*
as the kinds of things other people
want to keep in their homes
too
just in case
and just as likely to become
just more things one day
or things
for someone else's children to decipher

and argue over
or maybe
grip to their chests
as fresh panic
wells up, faces smeared
with such vile things
such grubby little
things
like
spots
and flecks
of desperation
and most of them
sick inside, bloated with hope
because
maybe the kinds of things
that hitchhiked
from family
to family in brown shoeboxes
or tissue paper
and
sometimes in local newspapers
too
papers
that sat
jammed full
of other moments
from other people's families,
that such things
would be the only things
worth keeping,
these few surviving things
that started out as my things
but so quickly

changed
until there was
not even a single thing
about me
left
attached
to even a single one of them.

chicken-bone

and you're back, of course you are
like a chicken-bone satellite in my head
digging through the grey
and splattering
everything for just a glimpse of pearl
which, when you find
you can clip
and re-arrange,
salting the earth as you leave
diminishing
every word
stuck on my tongue

and now your rooms
begin to slither and shrink around me
snug

until finally
mutely
I push back in a storm of junk food wrappers,
crappy little cape
aswirl as I
swing
and slash
in sand-castle heroics
pitting my pitiful plastic sword
against your might
a kind of guaranteed resurrection

on the cards
if I can just learn
      however it is that
           you are tamed

all my angst, once buried in little
           nods
           and distance, now fades
           because
           I snatch at any space
           free from voices
           and even kind faces
           and
           bury them
           with the car window
           down
           just a sliver as I get away,
           and sometimes
           it's no more than
           twenty-something steps
           but somehow they
           always
           do the trick.

a chocolate robin hood

hey
> *yeah?*

slow down a bit
> *I'm okay*

well, I heard that you're meant to chew 30 times
for optimal digestion, that's all
> *like, meat?*

everything, apparently
> *I've got a cast-iron stomach. it's*
> *like a factory of acid*

sounds painful
> *well, that's not all that's in there.*
> *I've got those bio-things too. the*
> *blue things from that ad. look*
> *like germs*

do you mean probiotics?
> *sounds right*

they do look a little like germs, yeah. that's
pretty funny
> *well, we're hardly Abbot and*
> *Costello*

true. do you think the kids know who that is?
> *what do you consider a kid?*

too young to believe in black and white TV
> *believe in? like, the Easter Bunny?*

you ever think about the Easter Bunny?
> *not a lot*

isn't it a crazy idea – imagine a giant, stinking

rabbit dipped in pink, sneaking into your place
overnight and leaving cash beneath your pillow
– like, I always thought it'd wake me up, as a kid
ever touched a rabbit's foot – wouldn't the pads
feel chilly? and where'd it get the cash too – does
it rob the richer kids on its way between homes?
like the Robin Hood of chocolate!

                    I thought they had fur
huh?

                    you know, the under-part of their
                    feet
they have pads, don't they
                    like dogs?
yeah. so, who told you?
                    the truth about that stuff?

right

                    dunno. I guess I figured it out. no
                    big moment, just wondered how
                    the damn thing could get to
                    every joint in one night. lotta
                    houses in our town. seemed
                    pretty simple once I was old
                    enough
so you don't resent anyone, like your parents?
                    not for that.
yeah?

                    yeah. look, I think it's starting to
                    rain, I'd better get going
I can give you a lift
                    sweet, thanks
so where are we going?
                    just the bank
it never ends, huh?
                    not until one of us dies

I didn't know they were in trouble – stock market bullshit, I guess

> *could be*

I once met a guy who swore up and down that he was onto something big. he carried around this old four leaf clover sealed in plastic. said he picked it the day after Woodstock

> *the 99 one?*

maybe. could have been the original one. he was old enough but didn't have that laid-back hippy vibe

> *what's that like?*

I dunno. dope and communism, I guess

> *I always think of Manson for*
> *some reason*

he probably wasn't a hippy

> *I know but didn't he wreck the*
> *summer of love? him and that*
> *Rolling Stones gig? it's like that*
> *quote from that guy who Johnny*
> *Depp played in that movie. a*
> *great wave or something?*

haven't seen it

> *well, I think he was saying that*
> *all the hope faded near the end*
> *of the 60s, like an empty pool or*
> *something and that's when*
> *everyone became cynical again.*
> *like now*

I'm not sure I'm cynical

> *you gonna say you're a realist?*
> *like I've never heard that before*

not exactly, more that, I'm not surprised by as much anymore. the bad stuff, you know? but even with all that I still think people are good deep down

I used to think that and then I
> *lost my glasses as a kid*

someone steal them?
> *nope. broke 'em. just coz*

what did you do?
> *told the teacher and they said*
> *they'd figure it out but nothing*
> *ever happened coz the little prick*
> *that did it was the son of some*
> *big shot solicitor*

man, that sucks
> *yeah. ran in to the guy a few years*
> *back, actually*

you sort him out?
> *nah, he was too rich. like, if I'd hit*
> *him he'd have done me for assault*
> *and then I'd be worse off than I*
> *am now*

but you wanted to
> *you bet. but I reckon I still got*
> *him in the end*

how?
> *saw the way his little girl acted*
> *with him. didn't give him nothing*
> *– went straight to her mum*

what do you mean?
> *I mean that at least I get along*
> *with my kids. how about you?*

pretty good, yeah
> *so, you know what you're gonna*
> *tell them about the Easter Bunny*
> *and Santa?*

...
> *you could try that chocolate*
> *Robin Hood thing?*

I suppose I could for a little while. sooner or later
I've got to figure out something better though
               I say that to myself most days
about Easter?
               about everything
yeah?
               yeah.

milking

I am milkman
deep in the mud
filling every syllable
with detritus
after emotion has bled out
and heaved its guts into the street –
yet I am only there to take notes
with pencil-stubs
leering
greedy for more detail
to prick and prod
every bruise and pinch like the small-time
fatcat
office hero
whose very touch will taint
and linger
with the half-life
of high-grade plutonium,
I am there only
with cameras for eyes, see them snap down
on every colour
now
leeching it all while developing,
reducing everything
to something so much less
than before
right down to just
a few pecks at the keyboard
so that later,

I can spit it all across the screen
or the page, and maybe the internet too
so that strangers might find
some shred of similarity
or maybe
just pass right on by
with not even a snicker but instead
a heroic measure
of indifference
ten-tonnes of *something better to do*
so I can realise that I got so fucking dirty
now for nothing
so I'll know that what I wrote
I stole from myself
and
had to force myself to not care
about that, get the fuck over that
fast, real fast
and know that what I felt
then (and now) was always going to be
canon fodder
for a couple of bucks
here and there.

fresh fruit

you can pick any date you like
for the moment
rebellion was monetized on behalf of
multi-national corporations
and it's hard to skip over rock and roll
as an example
but the one I really like
has the fruit-company that was so good at
hiding its sweat-shops and suicides behind
glossy advertising
and bi-weekly new editions,
or the kids and bigger kids
who made up their white-washed street team
pushing communication
further and further into an act of fashion

and I used to hear the drones say

it's just my fandom!
I'm allowed to obsess! I'm allowed to be loyal!

and my favourite:

I love it because it's unique –
and all my friends have one

and shit yeah, one day it'll be cool
to hate a different trend
hate a different company

sure, and I can't really be too smug
for boycotting
just one of them,
when just about every other thing
I fucking own
is buried in the prints of a different despot

but Jesus Christ, please don't dance
for the piper
and try to tell me it's just a cool song.

everyone else

what kind of snapped plastic-spoon
comfort
can I draw from the idea
that everyone feels this way at some point:

a stranger sleeps on my side of the bed
eats the banana I was saving for breakfast
and a stranger
times his drive to work
so that he arrives exactly when I would
and we both take that mile-deep breath
before we cross the threshold,
getting ready to fake it
so good

is it really of comfort
to know everyone else experiences this?

this guy's an ocean of salt
he's a slug
he's a life-saving medical breakthrough
and a sign for hot cinnamon donuts,
he's the kind of perfect coffee
found in travel brochures only
and he's undiscovered gold
he's rat-shit
he's insightful questions on TV
and he's the pocket-lint of every revolutionary
imprisoned, maybe

he's bleeding from every orifice too
doing it on *my* behalf
because I've asked him to,
once upon a time
somewhere back there
then
when
I made a choice between
the soft-pillow-smile of the optimist
and survival

and that me, the sweet one, by god I'm sorry
we all know I let you down, buddy

but check out the deck of cards
left on the outdoor setting,
nice green plants
there
to go with the after-image
of cigarette smoke
pole-dancing
up the umbrella
and yeah, the deck's stacked
against us

but this new, other me
this joker
said he'll play for us
and claims he'll win too,
but we aren't allow to play even a single hand
from now on,
that's the rule
that's his deal, he said
and so we have to come up with something

soon
or let him play
but holy shit,
how can I let *him* be the one to wake up
in my bed tomorrow?

incendiary

how much can you hate a thing?
I'm wondering because tomorrow
I'm going to take in a ruler
and scales and see what I come up with:
a tonne of rotting pennies
maybe
or something bigger, the apocalypse of a
thousand elephant feet
or a coastline
maybe
of the entire continent[3]
or something
deeper,
if I drill down for dinosaur bones
swimming in hidden oil
and count the grooves left in the earth
count every layer
each earthworm
insect, mite
and every flipping atom too, if I
come up with something that way
maybe
satisfy the census too
or if I take another path – this time
the blistering volume
of how many times I have not
said
please fuck off and take your bullshit
with you

or the eternal rain gauge
that I carry around
ready to fill
with promises mutilated
by bureaucratic traffic,
it's the kind of drought
where relief
is not even myth but a mere echo
of the first sound
cast out
and now
only the long gnashing of teeth
will be uncovered.

generational stillness

it's one of those centre-strip
wishing wells
surrounded by lawns in increments of neat
neater, neatest
with nice old trees too, their bark gnarled
as if waiting for the pencil
of a still-life student

but when I lean over
it's just typical small-town grimness
with cigarette butts
half a foot deep
locked in that generational stillness –
grey water
strangling every dream

and maybe it's all the way across town
but I swear
that the graveyard
has sent its hoar-frost here to roost,
I can almost taste the down-payment it's made
on every kid I used to teach

how far the stars seem now
from the grill of a fast-food sweat shop
or the single-hinge backdoor
after daddy-o
puts in another nomination
for shitbag of the year

and I'm supposed to impress upon them
the ever-lasting importance
of proper essay structure?

on the way home I slaughter a thousand bugs
with my windscreen
and somehow it feels hopelessly right.

and they lined up two by two

1. spine so thin

I was sure you had stopped me
with your final pixels;
sure you had made me barren
of all poetry
found a way to fill my mouth with clay
before a single syllable
could be forced
into some semblance of shape

how quickly four years
became a hundred aborted poems
perished
all by shark attack
in sallow waters

my spine so thin

and how I wondered and doubt grew fat
and happy beside me,
a hog left to rut as it pleased
soiling every fucking page
eyes bulging
in rancid euphoria

and god damn, it seems the biggest fool
is the one
I let myself become

I
stopped

until today, I guess
this is tomorrow
just a little bit early
and it's another opportunity

isn't it, to go from breakdown
to autobahn?

2. *with no elegance at all*

yet still when I type and there's old Capote
leaning over me
snickering
that's not writing

and if I take a second
I have to suspect there's another spectre
at the faucet,
someone else wrenching it closed

stopping

whatever it was that let me care back then

gutting

every inclination to spread some ink now

confidence from a confidence-man leads to
doubt

I cannot work it out:

how to say it with words
when words no longer trust me

so let me just say it
(with no elegance at all)

I do not understand how
but so much of my confidence seemed tied
to your approval

and now that you've played your sleight of hand
how do I believe your kind words
how do I reconcile a generosity of spirit
with the darkness you cast
across a hundred other poets, more, I don't
know

3. softest blue

it's pathetic, isn't it? that I cannot find
confidence
to take a stand
over my work or yours
when so much of my day is trying to banish
doubt for others

and so now I must hope
that the first swallow of the season
will hear my cry
and lend me wings of the softest blue.

all things impossible loom

making lunch
with trembling limbs today,
the knife is a lead weight
and the fridge door

more like a combination safe

outside
someone's stuffing
hymns and vertigo
into my mailbox

and all things
impossible
seem to loom large
before firm ground

I give myself some sweet old
'toughen-up' style
advice
but end up
spitting most of it into the basin

because a piece of doubt always lingers,
untraceable
as glass in carpet

and I'm sure now

that all this is going direct-to-video

but I'm still taking steps, like teeth grinding

paper wings
right about to be tested.

you again

had I not stomped you down
deep into the past
to slumber
now most fitfully
between tar and the thin
bones of dead birds
and skin
and blood
and fur from every ruined kangaroo?

yet here you walk once again
proud Lazarus
sprouting
your wheezing cheeks
and spreading green ash and misery
across my every
moment

that heavy hand:
colour of mould
scent of midnight
bright
gorgon eyes
lurking behind each tick of the clock,
numbers sharp enough
to re-open familiar wounds

until
I transform down
into something
smaller
and smaller
now
so small that maybe
I slip between
the final stroke of the butterfly's wing
and the wringing
hands
of the bumblebee
trapped behind glass

or
maybe end up
huddled
like cattle before wind,
all my smiles
turning to frost.

admit one

we never argue over the details:

life is one giant hospital

cobwebs oversee everything
and we seek out softness only in degrees now –

needle, dosage, frequency
side effect
& long-term damage

we must force ourselves to admit
that stasis is better than regression

and of course we're made to justify
self-preservation too –

snowblind on sugar
I cope in the loosest possible sense of the word

as together we build a pitiful sand castle
out of the scraps

and fill the moat with empty pill casings.

pale wings

I cannot find home
here
it seems it lacks, most utterly
lacks
a few things that lock in my mind
from those other places, things that somehow
make it to the new address:
warmth
not from the sun
but from patterns of sunlight on the wall
early morning
pale wings
from certain angles
or the deep afternoon orange blush
or the scent of eucalypt
almost-burning
and
sometimes, I can draw stuff like that
up from the grey
myself,
sometimes it's as simple
as being still
late at night when only two-rooms across
the hum of the fridge
is left to
keep time,
and by whatever accident
my mind grows still too
because all the restlessness has fallen out

and behind,
in the space that was once
occupied by a squirming mass of notes-to-self
there it is,
there's clean glass
and the sill
too
both waiting
for me
to go and rest my hands there.

a million times

that year the dragonflies
were big
hover-boards
that no-one could ride

and the sun was so hot
that we stayed
in the shade
like young sultans
and hopped across the concrete

only when we had to

back and forth to the milk bar
for ice-cream
and soft drink
at least a million times.

smaller and smaller

used to be a logging town

place for the hippies
to hide their dope crops

and maybe now it's a little more
or less
the same

only the bakery's been playing musical chairs
with the hairdresser
and one of the mechanic shops
is closed now

the general store lives on
in the shadows of trendy cafes
that always pop up
when you're
'just out of town'
not exactly overnight
but in 18 years something had to change, right?

on the other hand
some things stay the same:

rev-heads still measure theirs
with decibels
and burnt rubber

or fishtails beside the playground

gossip lingers too
as new faces weave old, old words
into the carpet

rust still grows on post boxes

families hoard picnic tables

and round the bend
the river's far too thin
for ghosts
now

and finally at night, late enough
at night
for the migrating trucks
to fill the highway
in lines of blazing red

I hear the faint roar
of memory
and the sweet slow magic of childhood
comes rushing back.

special occasions

after high school
we line up right on the edge

little wings aching

so fucking ready
to paint the sky with the afterburn
of our dreams, ripped right out of the packet
and devoured:

juices
running free and
the taste of certainty not yet gone bitter

I hear there's a reunion coming up soon
and I have no idea what to say
there
to the ones who fled, the ones who tore holes
in the road out of town
or the other ones who stayed
and had their feathers mulched in suburban
lawn-mowers
and normal, everyday mortgages
nor the ones like me who pretended that a trip
here and there
meant
they hadn't crashed back down to earth
to find a special kind of death –

the routine
panic
of paycheque to paycheque
until it sounds just like breathing,

or maybe a greatest hits package
or the swish of a flashy suit
that you can trot out
for funerals, birthdays
weddings
or right now, when you
have to fake it
for a room full of strangers.

risk

I let myself start remembering

how the garden hose, turned low
made a river
beside the brand-new concrete driveway
and the years before,
when all was dirt
are now overlooked
in favour of my brother and I
playing cars
then

sometimes I make the mistake
of going back there
and the new paint
high fence
and smaller plants
do their damage; that overlay bullies
the pure memory
until I rush to a photo album
and realise we were both wrong

I try to pin down
something exact:
the spot where lino met carpet
the maybe three or four
burn marks just beside the hearth,
or that old TV – did it really have a dial

in silver and black
and just how rough was the white noise
between clicks?

I'm seeking these details now
in the hope of finding something
irrefutable
because maybe that's what I need
to finally nail it all down,
now that everything has started
changing
at the speed of light.

young pine

ten years ago I could mark death
in abstract eventualities:
make a will, leave something
worthwhile behind, worry about
what specific form of cancer
will, according to the statistics, end up
getting me
and consider (in a slammed-door-kind-of-way)
how it might feel
to wake
and not have you beside me

but today I saw a young pine tree
that stretched for blue sky
and knew that
when I was gone it would be stern and tall,
that new feet would seek its shade
or shelter
from piercing rain

and it was just so different to being
thundered into silence
by the glitter of galaxies above

like a soft word from tomorrow
telling me
no need to try so hard.

thieving light

the thieving light of evening
takes all other details
elsewhere,
leaving behind
only an Impressionist's
precise blurring
of edges

and I hover
between kitchen and couch

waiting for new fireflies
to stick in the sky,
waiting for the moon
to restart
peace and quiet

and remember

how a strand of your hair
might gleam
in silver

or the scent of clean skin
like an empty bath

or the way
I can actually hear your happiness

without even a word
whenever
you click the kettle on

and hot water begins to sing.

ready? go

parachuting down
on dandelion spores
the sun
lifts my chin
and you smile too,
as all around us the weeds
begin to migrate

they pack up their thorns
and head
somewhere dark and cold
for a while
sure to return, but for now
it's enough to know
they're leaving

and so we set out
at last
really put the foot down
really
feel it in our chests too

that surging feeling

it's *escape*
when for so long
our two-lane town
has been the only thing

left after the night
is done,
and so we hum along
to the engine's baritone,
see ahead
to something better
to something
not quite panic either,
just the thrill
of uncertainty –
like

like
the highway had burst
all of its arteries
at once
like somehow
the green fields
had managed to keep
everything in shape
too

and the whole sky
is reflected
streaking
and sparkling in the many
drops of dew
that go
flying
across our windscreen.

pink tickets

how a scent
can change so much,
just a trembling of spring
in the leaves
and I can finally exhale
after a long, spindly winter
whose fingers
never really unwrapped
themselves
from around our spines
pulling
and dragging us
from cave to cave

and we have waited
on bramble-legs
now
unfolding from
where they've been
packed away like matches,
struggling
to breathe, slowly turning
into whispers of char
that filter down between
couch cushions

and the change is just so
welcome

like a crest of paint
crashing over canvas

hair desperately
alive

and paper-lantern streets
lined with white
blossoms
and pink tickets

I want to
bleed up the gravel path
and mark your front door

I want to harvest you all at once
with just one glance

and run
and skip and spin
and fling things into the air
high enough
that they somehow just stick there
and only much, much
later
begin to drift back down
to this hemisphere

until all that remains
up there
is the sweet pulp of the night.

swoon

when you come home

I am shoving the old calendar
face-first
into the sink
as the light fixtures swoon

hope is tactile
but you gotta be careful with it too:

it buries the front step
in feathers

and sends you two towns over
looking for
the only thing you left behind

but still – when you're here
beetles
moonwalk
and the fruit bowl
quickens
and finally, I find I can

smile at every thing.

mark each other

we're supposed to mark each other
you know
exactly how it goes, you know
it's one of those rules
that govern Life,
the ones that offer a tarnished
kind of comfort
in their supposed iron-cladding
like the ones
that only get fulfilled
in the cosy narratives of midday movies
and Disney
or any given summer's
feel-good
hit

and you know
all of this
the way you knew it before we met
but you're still like me
and you know
it's not like that on the other side of the screen

or at least it doesn't
have to be
and so instead of marks
we have always tried to leave behind
the kind of thoughts

that if we care to look up and see them

will burn
their afterimage
across the entire sky.

tinkerbell

maybe we can only tinker with life
and never revitalise it,
never get to ride off into the sunset
either

instead

just find ourselves consigned to a long series
of minor adjustments,
instead
simply maintain the rut
like a gutter gone to green

wake
to the spectre
of rainbows long since gone to ash
and falling
and settling to the earth
like little graveside offerings –

yet on the other hand

I still cling to his robes
and manage to drag him back
just a few steps

because defiance
matters

and because I know
I am sure
now
that a hundred small things
will always become something bigger.

from *stepping over seasons*

small town

has an old Esso sign on a tin shed
and someone who used to sell honey
painted yellow on the next one,

at the corner a pink golf ball
towers over the coastline, ridges
like the moon.

in spring flowers grow
round the blue tractor
and dirt collects in the seat

marks on the footpath
don't fade and the cemetery
never shrinks, only the town around it.

beyond the tennis courts
ghosts shed fingernails and
police sirens skip over fences;

no-one lives down there
where the surf plays dead
and moonlight walks on water.

from *between giants*

ridges in the skin

it's doubtful that the sour woman
in the gelato shop
was in a mood
because of the thousands
of Capuchin monks
and poor Romans
buried across the street

she'd be used to looking
over to the doors

where five chambers
of pelvic bones,
vertebrae and shoulder blades
made into wings
and skulls stacked
in seven-foot cages
lay

where beside them in a small chapel
not even a knuckle bone

and where mass must wait
until we tourists
stumble back
to our warm hotels
with slack faces
and a lingering chill,
very much aware of the marrow
beneath our skin.

from *old stone*

shuffling over old stone
the echo
of tour guides

shadows on the courthouse
shouting
over the pram

you are trying to sleep
and I am Coltrane's sax
steeped in sound

from *VI*

Campo de' Fiori

I chase you through the file extensions
littered across my computers
and with each little
click
you are enlarged
but I get no closer, salt in a wound
as the pixels
run
and I hit that X again
only to repeat the whole game
the next night,
in an aching chair
where moths are on loop
and the counterfeit moon
flickers
from inside the light shade,
it seems
now
that whenever I blink
you slip between the frames

and even in memory you fragment
as if the wind had been everywhere first:

gone

the taxi driver's face
but not his cigarettes
            gone

the rainbow of fruit but not the sun
where it punished Bruno's hood
and gone
the hundreds of cats
yet not the graffiti
worming
its way across yellow walls
                              gone
the tourists
but never the things we worshipped.

Also by Ashley

pollen and the storm
stepping over seasons
orion tips the suacepan
between giants/old stone
7 years
VI
teeth of the world
the afterburn of dreams (forthcoming)